WILDWORLD

Giant Pandas

Karen Dudley

A & C Black · London

First published in Great Britain in paperback in 2001 by
A & C Black (Publishers) Ltd, 35 Bedford Row, London WC1R 4JH.
First published 1997 in Canada by Weigl Educational Publishers Limited

ISBN 0-7136-5746-4
A Cataloguing in Publication Data (CIP) record of this book is available from the British Library.

Printed and bound in Canada

Project Editor
Lauri Seidlitz

Design and Illustration
Warren Clark

Project Coordinator
Amanda Woodrow

Editor
Kathy DeVico

Copy Editor
Janice Parker

Layout
Chris Bowerman

Consultant
Dr Don Reid, formerly with the WWF and WCI on panda research, now a Wildlife Inventory Specialist in British Columbia, Canada.

Acknowledgments
The publisher wishes to thank Warren Rylands for inspiring this series.

Special thanks to Nancy Nash for her advice and encouragement.

Photograph Credits

Calgary Zoological Society: cover, pages 14, 21, 37, 61 (Brian Keating), 33 far left (Chris Junck), 4, 10, 34, 53; **Corel Corporation**: pages 13, 43; **National Zoological Park/Smithsonian Institute**: pages 7, 15, 23, 26, 41, 59, 60 (Jessie Cohen), 5, 11, 12, 17, 18, 22, 30, 33 middle left, 42, 45, 46, 51, 56; **Don Reid/WWF**: pages 6, 9, 16, 24, 27, 28, 29, 32, 33 middle right, 36, 40, 44, 54, 57; **Tom Stack and Associates**: page 33 far right (Gary Milburn).

Contents

Introduction

Although giant pandas are most often described as cuddly, the panda is actually a powerful animal with a strong bite.

Giant pandas are often described as cute, cuddly, and lovable. The giant panda's short, flat nose, rounded ears, chubby body, and seemingly enormous eyes have made it a favourite animal for many people around the world. However, giant pandas are also wild creatures that have developed a unique way of surviving in the world.

In this book, you will find out what giant pandas eat. You will learn how giant pandas can communicate, even without seeing one another. You will discover how mother pandas and their tiny cubs survive in their wet mountain habitat. You will also find out why giant pandas have such unique black-and-white markings.

Features

Giant pandas have strong cheek muscles and huge teeth that are perfect for chewing up tough vegetation.

Opposite: Most of the giant panda's time is spent finding and eating bamboo.

Although the giant panda's heavy body and pigeon-toed walk make it seem clumsy at times, the panda is surprisingly flexible. It can even touch its head with its hind feet.

Giant pandas have many special adaptations that help them survive in their forested mountain habitat. They have thick, waterproof fur to keep them warm, and long, sharp claws to climb trees. Giant pandas have strong cheek muscles and huge teeth that are perfect for chewing up tough vegetation.

Take a close look at a picture of a giant panda. Is it more like a bear or a raccoon? This is a question that still puzzles many scientists. The giant panda has so many similarities to both that scientists cannot agree. As you learn more about the giant panda's features, perhaps you can decide for yourself.

Size and Body Shape

An adult giant panda weighs about 90 to 135 kilograms. On all fours, it stands almost one metre tall at the shoulder, and measures about 1.5 metres in overall length. Males are about 10 per cent larger than females.

The giant panda's body shape is well adapted to its forested environment. Strong front legs and heavy, powerful shoulders make giant pandas excellent climbers, which helps them escape danger. Pandas also need to be flexible so they can move easily through dense bamboo.

Giant pandas have short legs, and they travel very close to the ground. This makes them very slow walkers. Even when a giant panda is in danger, the fastest it can move is a slow, clumsy-looking trot.

LIFE SPAN

The life span of giant pandas in the wild is about 20 years. Wild pandas face many dangers, including accidents, disease, and food shortages. Sometimes they are hunted by humans, leopards, wild dogs, and other predators. Captive giant pandas may live to be 25 to 30 years old.

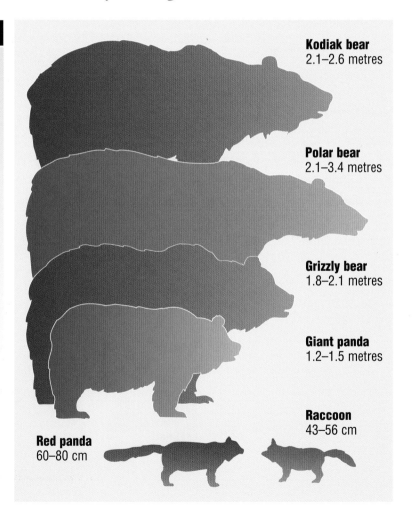

Kodiak bear
2.1–2.6 metres

Polar bear
2.1–3.4 metres

Grizzly bear
1.8–2.1 metres

Giant panda
1.2–1.5 metres

Raccoon
43–56 cm

Red panda
60–80 cm

Fur

Although a giant panda's fur looks soft and silky, it is actually quite thick and wiry. The hair of an adult giant panda can grow up to 10 centimetres in length. Each hair is coated with an oily substance that keeps the panda's fur dry. The giant panda's dense, oily fur helps to keep it warm in its chilly, wet habitat.

The black-and-white markings of the giant panda are unique among mammals. Their ears, shoulders, legs, and eyespots are black. The rest of their fur is creamy white. There are several theories about why the giant panda has such unusual markings. Some biologists believe the panda's colours are useful for **camouflage**. In the bamboo forests, patterns of light and shadow can make it difficult to see the giant panda's black-and-white markings. Other scientists believe the giant panda's colours are more useful for winter camouflage when snow covers the ground. Some scientists think the black-and-white fur helps the giant panda keep a steady body temperature. While the black fur absorbs heat from the sun and warms the panda, the white fur reflects the sun and cools the panda.

The giant panda's black-and-white fur can make it difficult to spot in its natural environment.

Another theory is that the giant panda's markings help it avoid other pandas. Like many other creatures, giant pandas will threaten an intruder by staring at it. The giant panda's large, black eyespots make their eyes look much bigger, so their stare appears to be more aggressive.

Special Adaptations

Giant pandas eat mostly bamboo, which is a sturdy kind of grass. Thick stalks of bamboo are very difficult to eat, but giant pandas have developed features that are specially adapted for their diet.

Face

When you look at the round face of a giant panda, you might think that it looks a little chubby. In fact, the giant panda's face is not fat, but gets its shape from massive cheek muscles. These extremely strong muscles help pandas chew their bamboo diet. The giant panda's jaw is also very heavy and strong. A giant panda's jaw and cheek muscles are so powerful that a panda could easily chew an aluminium dish into tiny pieces.

The giant panda's throat has a special lining to protect it from bamboo splinters.

Paws

Giant pandas have five fingers and toes, and long, sharp claws that allow them to climb trees easily. Their front paws have another special feature. The giant panda has a special "thumb" that sticks out from its palm. This is actually a wristbone that has grown and developed into a useful tool. It is **opposable**, which means it sits opposite to the rest of the panda's fingers, and can be pinched up against them. A panda can grasp a bamboo stalk by wrapping its fingers around the stalk and squeezing its "thumb" in to secure its hold.

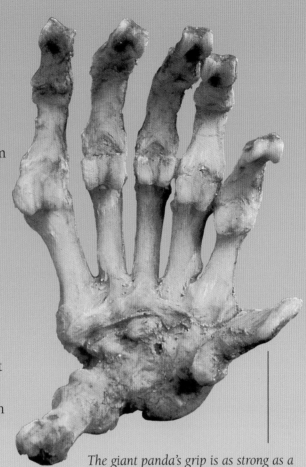

The giant panda's grip is as strong as a human's grip, because of a sixth finger. Without this secure hold, the panda would have trouble eating bamboo.

Teeth

Giant pandas have 42 teeth. Their teeth are wide and flat with ridges, and they are well adapted for crushing and chewing. Like humans, giant pandas have two sets of teeth during their lifetime. The giant panda has a much larger skull and teeth than the brown bear, although both animals eat mainly vegetation. The panda's large teeth evolved to help the animal eat tough stalks of bamboo.

Classification

There is only one species of giant panda (*Ailuropoda melanoleuca*). Wild giant pandas live only in small pockets of land in southwestern China.

Bear or Raccoon?

The question of whether the giant panda is more like a bear or a raccoon has a long history. In 1869 French naturalist Père David introduced the giant panda to the western world. He said the panda was a new kind of bear. Père David called it *Ursus melanoleucus*, which means "black-and-white bear". He sent a giant panda skeleton to his scientist friend, Alphonse Milne Edwards. Alphonse examined the bones, and decided that the giant panda looked more like a red panda. The red panda, sometimes called a firecat, is related to raccoons. Alphonse renamed the giant panda *Ailuropoda melanoleuca*, which means "black-and-white catfoot".

The Chinese name for the giant panda combines the theories of both Père David and Alphonse Milne Edwards. The Chinese call giant pandas daxiongmao (dah-shung maow), which means "large bear cat".

Raccoon.

Some scientists were unhappy with the new name given by Alphonse. They still believed the giant panda was more closely related to bears than to raccoons. Giant pandas look very like bears. They have similar brains, ear bones, and respiratory systems. They walk like bears, and, like bears, give birth to tiny cubs.

Other scientists believed that giant pandas were more closely related to red pandas, which are more like raccoons than bears. These scientists looked at the similarities between giant pandas and red pandas. Unlike some bears, red pandas and giant pandas do not **hibernate**. A giant panda's teeth and skull, and the colour pattern of its fur, resemble those of the red panda. Giant pandas and red pandas eat the same foods and live in the same kind of habitat.

Scientists debated the question for many years. In the 1980s, they conducted **genetic testing**. This is testing that examines **genes** to learn more about an animal's origin and its relationship to other animals. Some tests showed that the giant panda was a bear. Other tests indicated that it was a raccoon.

It is possible that giant pandas and red pandas are not closely related to either bears or raccoons. Instead, they may be a different kind of animal altogether. In his book, *The Last Panda*, biologist George Schaller concludes that the giant panda is simply a panda.

Black bear.

Social Activities

By observing giant pandas in the wild, biologists discovered that pandas are solitary creatures.

Opposite: Like most bear species, giant pandas usually spend their time alone.

Giant pandas in zoos often have more contact with other pandas than they would in the wild.

Presently, there have been only two studies done on the giant panda's social life. One study was conducted on the Wolong Natural Reserve in the Sichuan province of southwestern China. By observing giant pandas in the wild, biologists discovered that pandas are **solitary** creatures. Except during the mating season, giant pandas usually try to avoid direct contact with other pandas. Each panda rarely leaves its own territory, so giant pandas do not usually need to defend their territory.

To help stay out of one another's way, pandas have developed a complex system of communication. This helps them avoid direct conflict with one another.

Female Home Ranges

Each female giant panda has her own **home range**. Within this range, females usually have a favourite area where they spend most of their time. This area, called a core range, may be as small as 40 hectares in size. The core range is centred around the best bamboo patches in her territory. While a female might allow another female into her home range, she will not allow another female into this favourite core area. Sometimes a male giant panda may share the same range as a female. Unless it is mating season, however, the pandas will try to stay away from one another. Female pandas only share their range with their own cubs.

The size of a giant panda's home range depends mostly on how much bamboo is available in the area. A female panda must ensure she has a range with enough bamboo for herself and her cubs.

Male Home Ranges

The home ranges of male giant pandas may overlap the ranges of several females, and may come into contact with the ranges of other males. The only time males will seek out a female is during the mating season. Unlike female pandas, males do not have a favourite part of their home range. They spend much of their time travelling throughout their entire range.

When males meet other males during their travels, they rarely show aggression towards one another. Male pandas do not try to defend their territory. They are usually more concerned with establishing their rank than they are with protecting their home ground. A higher-ranked male panda has a better chance of mating than a lower-ranked panda.

Male giant pandas determine their social rank by comparing their size and strength with other males. Weaker pandas give way to the larger, stronger pandas.

Although a giant panda doing a handstand looks very odd, pandas do this to leave their scent and mark their territory. Other pandas will smell the mark and know they are near another panda's home range.

The Mating Season

Giant pandas are more active during the mating season, which takes place from mid-March to mid-May. During this season, giant pandas spend much of their time looking for mates. They call out more often, and leave **scent marks** on the stumps and logs in their home range.

Giant pandas can be very noisy during the mating season. Their loud calls will often echo throughout the forest. Female scent marks and vocal calls, such as moans, bleats, and barks, will attract sometimes as many as four or five males at a time. The male pandas will often fight each other for the chance to mate with the female. The female may climb up a tree to avoid the conflict.

The entire mating process takes only about two or three days. Apart from the time a cub spends with its mother, this is the only time that giant pandas socialise with other giant pandas. Once they have mated, female and male giant pandas go their separate ways.

It is hoped that giant pandas born in zoos can someday be released back into their natural habitat in China. However, zoo breeding programmes are generally not successful because the pandas are not living in their natural social environment.

Naturalists Talk About Giant Pandas

George Schaller

"Years have passed since I last saw giant pandas in the wild, yet their powerful image continues to impinge on my life. Pandas are creatures so gentle and self-contained that they still affect me by the force of their uniqueness, by their aura of mystery."

George Schaller is a world-renowned giant panda biologist. Working out of the Wolong Natural Reserve in China, he was part of a team that conducted an important study on giant pandas living in the wild.

Keith and Liz Laidler

"Although the giant panda lives only in China, in a very real sense it belongs to the whole world... if we can allow a creature as loved and cherished as the giant panda to vanish from the face of the earth, what hope is there for the rest of the natural world?"

Keith and Liz Laidler are zoologists and wildlife filmmakers. They are active in wildlife conservation efforts, and they have produced a film entitled *Pandas of the Sleeping Dragon*, about the giant pandas on the Wolong Natural Reserve.

Don Reid

"[Saving giant pandas means] much more than just dollars and cents. They touch our spirit in a much more fundamental way – hence their ability to evoke such wonder and awe."

Don Reid is a biologist and leading giant panda expert. He has studied the pandas of the Wolong Natural Reserve with George Schaller and Chinese panda expert Hu Jinchu.

Communication

Giant pandas use body language to communicate when they are face-to-face with other pandas. Since pandas avoid direct contact as much as possible, they more commonly use other ways of communicating. Giant pandas communicate by using a combination of different vocal calls, and by leaving scent marks.

Scent Marking

Like human fingerprints, each panda's odour is different from every other panda's odour. Pandas rub the glands on their hindquarters against something to leave an oily liquid as their mark. Pandas can tell the gender and age of another panda by its scent mark. They can also tell how long ago the panda made the mark. If the mark was left by a female, other pandas can even tell if she is ready to mate.

There are a variety of ways for a panda to leave its scent mark. Sometimes the panda will use its whole body to rub its smell well in.

SCENT-MARKING METHODS

Lifted Leg
- The panda lifts its leg and rubs its hindquarters against an object.

Squat
- The panda squats on its hind legs and rubs its hindquarters on a stump or log.

Handstand
- The panda backs against a tree or large rock, balances on its front paws, and leans its legs against the surface as it marks.

Giant pandas call more often during the mating season.

Body Language

Unlike humans, giant pandas do not make faces to show their moods. Instead, giant pandas communicate by holding their bodies in certain ways. When a giant panda wants to threaten another, or show its superior rank, it lowers its head so that its eyespots and ears are visible. Sometimes it will even bob its head up and down, or swat at the other panda with its forepaws. A submissive or lower-ranked panda turns its head to avoid eye contact. It may drop its head completely and cover its eyespots with its paws. The lower-ranked panda may even roll on its back.

Calling

Giant pandas can make 12 distinct sounds. They combine these sounds in complex combinations that vary in loudness. Each sound has a certain meaning. Sounds are mixed to communicate the panda's mood.

SOUND/CALL	MEANING
Growl, roar	Aggression or threat
Huff, snort, chomp, honk	Anxiety or worry
Moan, bark, yip, squeal	Excitement
Bleat	Friendliness
Squawk	This is a sound made by young pandas in distress.

Panda Cubs

The first month of a cub's life is spent almost entirely in the arms of its mother.

Giant panda cubs are usually born at the end of the summer, when bamboo is most abundant. The mother needs to have a good food supply so she can stay strong enough to look after her cub. Male pandas leave after mating, and the mother panda raises her cub on her own. Giant panda mothers are well known for the care they give to their young. The first month of a cub's life is spent almost entirely in the arms of its mother. The mother panda nurses her cub, and keeps it warm, dry, and clean.

Opposite: Giant panda cubs get their familiar black-and-white markings within a few weeks after birth.

Efforts to breed giant pandas in zoos are sometimes unsuccessful, just as cubs born in the wild sometimes do not survive.

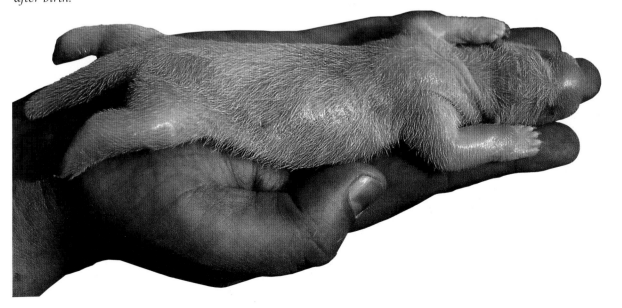

23

The Den

Giant panda cubs are usually born in August or September. A few days before giving birth, the mother panda searches for a good place to make a den. Giant pandas like to build their dens in the hollow stumps of large evergreen trees. They may also build a den in a dense patch of bamboo, or in a large crack in a rock. The dens are built close to good sources of food and water. The den must keep the mother and her new cub warm and dry. To make the den more comfortable, the mother giant panda lines it with twigs, wood chips, and even young trees.

Trees or caves provide the mother giant panda with a safe place to give birth to her cubs.

The Birth

The **gestation period** for giant pandas can vary from 97 to 163 days. The reason for this variation is a process called **delayed implantation**. After the mother giant panda becomes pregnant, the cub does not start to grow immediately. The cub will only start growing if the mother panda is able to get enough food. Once the cub begins to develop, it takes about 45 to 60 days before it is born.

A giant panda usually gives birth to a single cub. Sometimes twins are born. When this happens, the mother often ignores the weaker cub. She does not have enough energy to care for two cubs.

Care

Giant panda mothers are very attentive. As soon as the cub is born, the mother panda picks it up and holds it close to her body to keep it warm. For the first month, the cub stays tucked under her chin, snuggled beneath her arm, or cradled in her forepaw. When the mother needs to go out of the den to find food, she picks up her cub and carries it gently in her mouth. A mother giant panda sleeps sitting up, with her cub held carefully in her arms.

A giant panda carries her cub in the same way that a cat carries a kitten.

It is a good thing that giant panda mothers are so caring. A panda mother is 900 times larger than her newborn cub. At this ratio, a 3.5-kilogram human baby would have a mother that weighed more than 3 tonnes!

Although giant panda cubs are very small, they have extremely loud voices. Whenever a young panda is either uncomfortable or hungry, it squawks noisily. The mother responds immediately to her cub's cries. Even though giant pandas are usually very easygoing, a mother panda can be vicious if her cub is in danger.

Development

Weeks 1 – 4

A giant panda cub is helpless in its first month of life. A newborn panda is tiny, pink, blind, and toothless. It is completely dependent on its mother for food, warmth, and protection. Its eyes are closed, and it is unable to crawl. It is covered with only a thin coat of white fur that shows its pink skin underneath. Newborn giant pandas weigh only 56 to 140 grams, and measure only about 15 centimetres in length. After a week, the giant panda cub starts to grow its black-and-white fur.

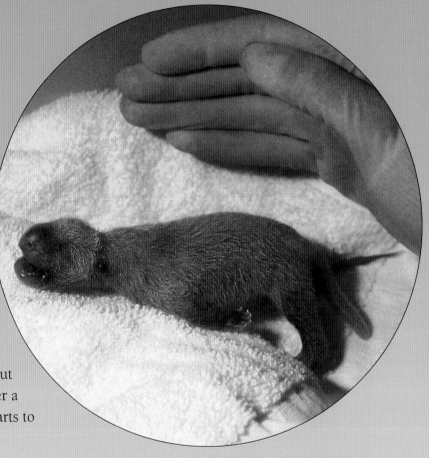

Weeks 5 – 11

After the first 6 weeks, a giant panda cub opens its eyes. Its fur is much thicker, and it is able to leave the den to travel with its mother. The giant panda cub grows quickly, but it is still dependent on its mother. She must carry it wherever she goes. At this age, a giant panda can only move around by wriggling or rolling from side to side.

The first giant panda ever to be born in captivity was born in a Beijing zoo in 1963. Since then, zoos in China and the rest of the world have worked hard to breed giant pandas.

Weeks 12 – 28

As the young cub continues to grow, it learns how to stand and walk on its short legs. It also develops its climbing skills by crawling all over its mother. A giant panda cub is very playful. After five months, the cub weighs about 10 kilograms. It begins to eat bamboo, although it will continue to suckle milk until it is eight or nine months old.

Weeks 29 – 52

After eight months, the young giant panda stops suckling milk and concentrates on eating bamboo. It is able to walk and climb by itself, but the cub still depends on its mother for protection. During this time, the giant panda learns how to communicate with other pandas, and how to survive in its environment. Some cubs leave their mothers after about 18 months, while others stay until they are two-and-a-half years old. Giant pandas are not ready to mate until they are five or six years old.

Giant panda cubs are good tree climbers, and will sometimes climb a tree to avoid danger.

Habitat

Giant pandas are found only in the Chinese provinces of Sichuan, Gansu, and Shaanxi.

Opposite: Giant pandas are well adapted to wet forests because their main food source, bamboo, grows best in areas where there is a lot of moisture.

Giant pandas live in misty, cloud-covered forests, high in the mountains of China. These forests are very damp and rainy. In one year, a forest may receive up to 127 centimetres of rain and snow.

A habitat is the place where an animal lives, grows, and raises its young. Giant pandas are not well adapted to live in most habitats. Giant pandas are found only in the Chinese provinces of Sichuan, Gansu, and Shaanxi.

Giant panda territories must contain a lot of bamboo to eat, thick bushes for shelter, and large, hollow fir trees for building dens. It is also very important for giant pandas to have a good source of drinking water nearby. If water is far away, the pandas would use too much energy trying to get a drink. Giant pandas will ignore an otherwise ideal range if the only water source is more than a kilometre away. A giant panda's home range within its habitat can vary in size from about 3.5 to 23 square kilometres, depending on how much bamboo is available.

Seasonal Activities

Giant pandas spend most of their time searching for food and eating. The giant panda's seasonal movements are directly affected by the availability of bamboo. If bamboo is available, pandas travel as little as possible. In one month, they may only visit 10 per cent of their range.

In spring and summer when bamboo shoots are tender and rich in protein, pandas eat as many of them as possible. During the summer, bamboo produces more leaves, so pandas eat more of this new greenery. In searching for shoots and leaves, giant pandas often move up and down the mountain slopes. This is because different types of bamboo grow in different areas on the mountain slopes.

When winter arrives, finding food becomes more difficult. Bamboo is an evergreen, which means it stays green throughout the colder months. However, it does not grow in the winter and loses many of its leaves. During the winter, pandas must eat more of the plentiful bamboo stems, which are not as nutritious.

Giant pandas do not hibernate because their bamboo diet will not allow them to build up enough fat reserves for the winter.

Viewpoints

Should giant pandas be kept in captivity?

Giant pandas are severely endangered due to habitat loss. As more mountain forests are cut down to build farms, wild giant panda populations are shrinking. Giant pandas survive outside of their natural habitat in several zoos and breeding facilities around the world.

1 Giant pandas are now so rare that zoos may be their only hope for survival.

2 Few studies have been conducted on wild giant pandas. Pandas live in remote areas, which makes it difficult for biologists to conduct research. Much of what we know about panda behaviour comes from studying captive pandas.

3 Giant pandas are needed for captive breeding programmes. We must have captive breeding programmes to make up for the low birthrate in wild panda populations. If captive breeding programmes are successful, the giant panda species can be preserved in zoos.

1 By keeping giant pandas in zoos, we are creating a demand for them. If one zoo has a giant panda, then other zoos may want one as well. This means that more wild pandas will be captured for zoos. Wild giant panda populations are already too small.

2 Studies of captive giant panda behaviour may not be very helpful in understanding wild pandas. Captive pandas living in zoos may behave very differently from pandas in the wild.

3 There is little or no cooperation between many of the zoos that currently have pandas. A good captive breeding programme does not exist. In some cases, captive pandas are never given the chance to mate. Giant pandas mate more easily and successfully in the wild.

Finding Giant Pandas

Even biologists who study giant pandas have trouble finding them. Giant pandas like to live where bamboo is abundant. Due to their body shape, they can crawl or push their way through the dense growth. Humans, however, often get stuck in bamboo when trying to track wild pandas.

To study giant pandas, biologists must first capture them. Biologists set traps that are baited with food. When the giant pandas go after the bait, the trapdoor closes. The biologists then use a **tranquilliser** to make the panda sleep. Once the giant panda is asleep, biologists can examine it. They often attach a radio collar to the panda's neck. The giant panda slowly wakes from the tranquilliser and is released back into the forest. The collar sends out signals that biologists use to track the panda. This process is called **radio tracking**.

This Chinese researcher is using a radio antenna to try to find a giant panda with a radio collar around its neck.

Disappearing Habitat, Disappearing Animals

China is home to many rare and unusual animals. Giant pandas share their habitat with many of these creatures, including the dhole, asiatic golden cat, leopard, musk deer, muntjac, and serow. By conserving giant pandas and their habitat, we can also conserve these other animals.

Here are four animals that share the same habitat as the giant panda. Below you will find information about each one. See if you can match the information with the animal.

A. Asiatic black bear **B.** Red panda **C.** Takin **D.** Golden monkey

1 *Food*: Eats the leaves and shoots of bamboo; also eats wild berries and other fruits in autumn.
Behaviour: Establishes a small home base; communicates through vocalisation and scent marking; dens in tree cavities.
Status: Endangered due to habitat loss.

2 *Food*: Eats mostly wild fruit, nuts, and shoots; sometimes eats insects.
Behaviour: Builds sleeping nests out of bamboo stems; hibernates through the winter; generally solitary except during the mating season.
Status: Endangered due to hunting; body parts used in traditional Chinese medicines.

3 *Food:* Eats grasses, herbs, leaves, and bark.
Behaviour: Lives in herds of ten to thirty-five; makes long migrations each season; likes dense, thorny vegetation where it can hide from danger.
Status: Endangered due to hunting and habitat loss.

4 *Food:* Eats leaves, fruit, lichens, and bamboo shoots.
Behaviour: Lives in trees in groups of up to 100 animals; shy of humans.
Status: Endangered due to hunting and habitat loss; body parts used in traditional Chinese medicine.

Answer Key: 1B, 2A, 3C, 4D

Food

Opposite: Much of the food that a giant panda eats is not digested. An adult giant panda eating a lot of food in the spring can produce approximately 28 kilograms of droppings in 24 hours.

Giant pandas will sometimes eat meat or the occasional spring flower, but its favourite food is bamboo. In fact, most of the giant panda's diet is bamboo. Bamboos are grasses with stems that grow for many years and can become quite woody and tall. In China, there are about 300 species of bamboo. Some species can reach heights of over 4.6 metres. There are about 25 different kinds of bamboo in the mountains where the pandas live. Pandas especially like to munch on umbrella bamboo, arrow bamboo, and golden bamboo.

BAMBOO

The **culm walls** are made of living tissue. In comparison, a tree's trunk is dead, except for the bark.

The **nodes**, or joints, in the bamboo stalk give it strength.

The **culm**, or stalk, is hollow and strong.

What They Eat

Giant pandas' eating habits are unusual. Although 99 per cent of their diet is bamboo, their digestive systems are designed for eating meat. A long time ago, giant pandas were **carnivores**, or meat-eaters. At some point in time, they switched over to eating bamboo, which is a far less nutritious food. Scientists are puzzled about why this happened. Pandas absorb only about 20 to 30 per cent of bamboo nutrients. Other plant-eaters, such as deer, absorb about 80 per cent of the nutrients in their food. The giant panda's highly specialised diet means it must eat for most of its waking hours to get enough nutrients to survive.

Sometimes giant pandas will eat other vegetation, such as horsetails, rushes, wild parsnip, willow leaves, and the bark from fir trees. They will even eat bamboo rats or other animals if they can either catch or scavenge them. Giant pandas like meat, which is very high in protein and nutrients. They cannot get it very often, however, because they are not very good hunters. Most of the meat they do eat is **carrion**, which is an animal that has died of natural causes, or that has been killed by another animal.

Pandas eat many varieties of bamboo. Each panda's diet varies according to the type of bamboo in its area, and the time of year. Pandas will usually eat only the most nutritious part of the bamboo available in each season. The umbrella bamboo shoots pictured here are about 2 metres high after four weeks of growing.

How They Eat

A giant panda can peel and eat a bamboo shoot in about 40 seconds.

On average, a giant panda eats 11 to 14 kilograms of bamboo in one day. During the spring, however, a panda may eat 45 kilograms of bamboo shoots in a single day. Pandas usually eat sitting or lying down. They grasp the bamboo shoot or stalk in their forepaws, and use their teeth to strip off the tough outer layer to get at the softer fibres inside.

Giant pandas eat every part of the bamboo that grows above the ground. In the spring, giant pandas eat the nutritious and tender bamboo shoots. These shoots are a high protein food source. During the rest of the year, giant pandas eat bamboo leaves and stalks. In the winter, there is little food available other than bamboo. Pandas usually eat for eight hours, sleep for four hours, and get up to start eating again.

The Problem with Bamboo

In some ways, bamboo is an ideal source of food for giant pandas because bamboo plants are usually very abundant. They grow in thick patches, and stay green throughout the cold months.

The biggest problem with bamboo comes from the plant's life cycle. All species of grass follow a cycle of growth, flowering, and seeding. Most grasses follow this flowering cycle on a yearly basis, but bamboo is different. Depending on the species of bamboo, its flowering cycles can take intervals of 30 to 120 years. Bamboo grows for most of this cycle, providing food for giant pandas.

When the bamboo reaches its flowering cycle, however, the entire species flowers, puts out seeds, and dies. This is called bamboo **dieback**. Whenever a bamboo dieback has happened in the past, giant pandas were able to **migrate** to another area that had a different kind of bamboo. Now, the giant panda has lost so much of its habitat to farms and other human activities that it may not be able to find another food source during a dieback. If this happens, many giant pandas may starve to death.

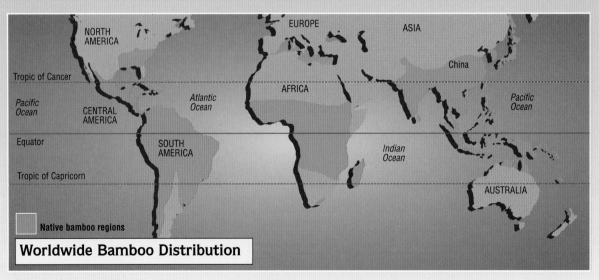

There are over 1,000 types of bamboo in the world. Some varieties are the size of field grass, and others grow to heights of 33.5 metres, with stalks 30 centimetres in diameter.

THE BAMBOO LIFE CYCLE

Shoots
- They appear in the spring or summer.
- Pandas eat as many shoots as they can because they are very nutritious.

Growth
- Pandas eat both the leaves and stalks.
- There is usually so much bamboo at this stage that pandas have plenty to eat.

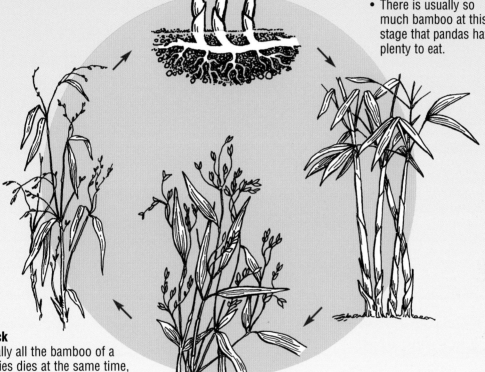

Dieback
- Usually all the bamboo of a species dies at the same time, no matter where it is growing in the world.
- It can take 10–15 years before bamboo grows back after dieback.

Flower
- Flowers have seeds that are spread by wind or animals.
- Different kinds of bamboo flower at different times.

Competition

The most serious competitors of the giant panda are humans.

Opposite: To deal with their large population, the Chinese have developed farming methods that use every available piece of land, including mountains that may have once been good panda habitat.

Giant pandas lead a solitary existence with one main purpose: getting enough food. This focus in a panda's life rarely puts it in conflict or competition with any other animals, including other pandas. They generally avoid or ignore other animals in their environment.

The most serious competitors of the giant panda are humans. Humans compete with pandas for land. Much of the habitat of giant pandas has been taken over by human activities.

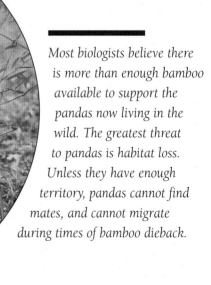

Most biologists believe there is more than enough bamboo available to support the pandas now living in the wild. The greatest threat to pandas is habitat loss. Unless they have enough territory, pandas cannot find mates, and cannot migrate during times of bamboo dieback.

Competing with Other Giant Pandas

It takes a lot of energy to compete for food, territory and mates. Giant pandas cannot afford the energy that it would take to compete with one another for these things. Bamboo is normally so plentiful that there is no need for giant pandas to fight over food.

Giant pandas also do not fight for territory. Their system of communication works well enough that they are usually able to avoid one another. Scent marks and other signs let intruders know that another giant panda has claimed an area. In this way, territorial disputes that could use up a lot of energy are easily avoided.

The only time giant pandas may compete with one another is during the mating season. If more than one male wants to mate with a female, they must decide which male is higher-ranked. Sometimes, these competitions can become aggressive, and the two males will wrestle, push, and bite. The winner becomes the higher-ranked giant panda, and will be the one to mate.

It is very rare to see more than one panda at a time in the wild.

Relationships with Other Animals

A giant panda is so large that it does not have many natural enemies. Weasels, marten, wild dogs, and leopards live in the bamboo forests. All of these predators will prey on giant panda cubs. This is one of the reasons why a mother panda keeps such a close watch on her cub. Sometimes, wild dogs or leopards will prey on an adult panda that is old or sick.

Besides the giant panda, only two other animals depend on bamboo for survival: red pandas and bamboo rats. When bamboo is abundant, there is almost no competition for food among these animals. When a species of bamboo dies back, the giant pandas, red pandas, and bamboo rats must all find another source of bamboo.

Adult giant pandas are so large that they do not have many natural enemies. Snow leopards, however, will prey on the more vulnerable panda cubs. Leopards may also try to kill adult giant pandas, especially if the panda is old or sick.

Competing with Humans

As human populations have grown, human activity has steadily spread up the sides of China's mountains. Some forests have been burned as fuel, while others have been cleared for agriculture. Many pockets of bamboo forest are now surrounded by open, cultivated land.

As their natural habitat is destroyed, giant pandas are crowding into increasingly smaller areas. Often these pockets of forest have only one species of bamboo. When all the bamboo in an area flowers and dies, giant pandas try to migrate to other areas where there are different kinds of bamboo still growing. If two bamboo forests are separated by farms or villages, the giant pandas cannot migrate, and may die of starvation.

The Chinese government is trying to stop or slow uncontrolled logging. In some places, peasants are given financial help to reduce the need to cut down more trees. In other places, researchers are trying to plant new crops of bamboo.

44

Decline in Population

Although it is against the law, many poachers believe it is worth the risk to illegally hunt pandas. One giant panda pelt, used to make a rug, can be sold for as much money as a rural farmer could make in ten years.

The pattern of fossil distribution shows that giant pandas once lived throughout China. They are now found only in a few small areas. Climate changes caused the bamboo to die off in the lower lands. When this happened, the pandas moved into mountainous regions where bamboo still grew.

Ancient climate changes explain why giant panda populations have shrunk in the past. At the present time, however, it is human activities that are mostly to blame for the decline of the species. Habitat loss, in particular, has severely affected the giant panda. Even before humans began taking over their lands, giant pandas often starved during times of bamboo dieback. As their habitat gets smaller, the number of giant pandas that die during these times increases sharply.

To make matters worse, many panda populations are now isolated from other panda populations by farms and fields. This is a problem during the mating season. If a female cannot find a male that she likes in her own territory, she cannot go to a different territory to find a mate. If she does not mate, one less panda cub will be born.

Another reason for the decline in giant panda populations is **poaching**. Giant pandas have been a protected species since 1939, but in the last few years, poachers have started to kill them for their pelts. Under Chinese law, poachers may be sentenced to death if they are caught.

Giant pandas face natural dangers as well. They can become ill, have accidents, or become infected with parasites. Parasites do not usually kill a panda, but they may stunt the panda's growth, or prevent it from mating.

Folklore

olklore, myths, and legends reflect the feelings we have about people, animals, and the world around us. In China, giant pandas are considered to be national treasures. It is a bit surprising, therefore, that pandas do not appear very often in Chinese folklore. This may be because giant pandas are shy creatures that were difficult to find. They lived in such remote areas that they were not often seen, and therefore not much was known about them.

It was not until the twentieth century that giant pandas became known to the rest of the world. They are now a popular subject for Chinese artwork and stories, and are also the subject of stories around the world.

"Big bear cat", the giant panda, written in Chinese characters.

Opposite: Giant pandas have become a popular subject for Chinese watercolour paintings.

Folklore History

Giant pandas were first mentioned in historical records about 1,200 years ago. Two hundred years later, giant pandas were the rare and treasured possessions of emperors and other people of great importance. An emperor from the Han Dynasty (202 BC to AD 220) kept a panda in his palace, and an emperor from the Tang Dynasty (AD 616 to 907) sent two pandas to the emperor of Japan as a goodwill gesture. In these old records, the gifts are called "white bears". Nobody knows for certain whether these white bears were actually giant pandas. It does makes sense, however, that an animal as rare as the giant panda would become part of an emperor's treasure.

Since the Tang Dynasty, the panda has been considered a rare treasure. In 1972 the Chinese government gave two pandas to the Smithsonian Institute's National Zoo in Washington, DC. The animals were given as a symbol of friendship between the Chinese and American governments.

A Tibetan Myth

Although giant pandas do not appear in many Chinese folktales, they do appear in a Tibetan myth. At the beginning of the story, four young shepherdesses are killed when they try to save a panda from a hungry leopard. When the other pandas hear what has happened, they decide to hold a funeral to honour the girls' sacrifice.

The story goes that giant pandas at this time were pure white, without a single black marking. To honour the deceased, the white pandas arrived at the funeral wearing black armbands. The pandas were so sad, and so moved by the ceremony, that they began to cry. As their tears rolled down, the dye from the black armbands began to run and mingle with their tears. As they rubbed their eyes, the black dye made big spots. In their grief, they clutched at their ears, and hugged one another closely. The black dye marked the areas where the giant pandas touched themselves and each other.

Although the pandas kept these black marks as a reminder of the girls, they also wanted their children to remember what happened. The pandas turned the four shepherdesses into a mountain with four peaks. This mountain stands in the Sichuan province near the Wolong Natural Reserve in China.

Stories About Pandas

Although pandas are rare in folktales, they do appear in other kinds of stories. Here are just a few you might enjoy:

In *Panda*, Jake travels to China with his father and some other scientists in search of some rare plants. He is longing to see a panda. One day, the men leave Jake at the camp and a panda finds its way into his tent. At first Jake is scared but when he offers the panda some food it is gentle. Jake takes a photo of the panda but as it leaves it knocks the camera and breaks it. When the scientists return they don't believe Jake's story – until the panda later returns to the camp. The book includes a fact sheet with information and details of how pandas are in danger and what you can do to help.

Allen, Judy. *Animals at Risk: Panda*. Walker
    Books, 1998.

Follow the adventures of Lu Yi as he finds and raises an orphaned giant panda named Su Lin. As Su Lin grows bigger, Lu Yi knows he cannot keep him. Find out what happens to Su Lin, and learn how Lu Yi discovers his life's work.

Schlein, Miriam. *Year of the Panda*.
    New York: HarperCollins, 1992.

In *Mr Chas and Lisa Sue Meet the Pandas*, Mr Chas and Lisa Sue discover a secret door in the pantry of Lisa Sue's New York home. To their surprise, the door leads to a long hallway where two talking pandas romp and play. As Mr Chas and Lisa Sue discover, the pandas like to dress up as dogs and go out to enjoy the city life. When the pandas decide to go to Paris, Mr Chas and Lisa Sue resolve to help them.

Lebowitz, Fran. *Mr Chas
    and Lisa Sue Meet the
    Pandas*. New York:
    Knopf, 1994.

Pandas in Popular Culture

In 1936 Su-Lin arrived at the Brookfield Zoo in Chicago. He was the first live giant panda to leave China. By 1939 eleven pandas had been taken from China to live in zoos around the world. As soon as people outside of China saw the cuddly-looking creatures, they went panda crazy!

Pandas began appearing on everything from figurines to earmuffs. There have been panda toys, mugs, place-mats, and even shower curtains. The black-and-white figure of the panda appears on shirts, posters, pins, bags and even ties. The panda craze also affected China. Giant pandas began appearing in Chinese paintings, paper art, and embroidery.

Popular culture includes art, music, and literature. In 1989 Roberta Stephen wrote a piece of music called the *Panda Suite* for cello and piano. Michael Foreman has written many children's books that feature a panda character. The Chinese government issued a series of postage stamps that show the giant panda, as well as other endangered animals. Giant pandas are now a familiar symbol of the Earth's wildlife heritage, and of human efforts to save it.

Su-Lin means "a little bit of something very cute". Ruth Harkness, without training or experience, became the first Westerner to capture and present a live giant panda to the world outside China.

The Distribution of Pandas in China

Present distribution

Approximate distribution in the 18th century

Approximate prehistoric distribution

MONGOLIA

NORTH KOREA

SOUTH KOREA

Beijing

CHINA

SHAANXI

Xi'an

GANSU

Shanghai

Chengdu

Chongqing

SICHUAN

TAIWAN

INDIA

Tropic of Cancer

Hong Kong

MYANMAR
(BURMA)

VIETNAM

LAOS

Status

There are only about 1,000 giant pandas living in the wild today.

Only 15 giant pandas live in zoos outside of China. Promotional material produced by zoos draw many people to see these unusual animals. Zoos believe that displays help educate people about the need to save the panda from extinction.

I n the mid-1970s, many giant pandas died of starvation because of a widespread bamboo dieback. Suddenly people realised that they knew very little about these rare animals, and they began to ask questions: how do they live? Why do they starve during the dieback? How many giant pandas are left?

These questions prompted extensive studies on the giant panda, as well as a count of the giant panda population. This count took three years to complete, from 1985 to 1988. When the results were in, it was obvious that giant pandas were in serious trouble. There are only about 1,000 giant pandas living in the wild today. An additional 100 pandas live in Chinese zoos, circuses, and breeding facilities.

Crisis and Rescue

In the mid-1970s, at least three species of bamboo on the Min Mountains flowered and died. Many giant pandas starved to death as a result. When bamboo on the Qionglai Mountains began flowering and dying in 1983, many feared the same thing would happen.

China organised a huge rescue effort to save the pandas from starvation. Refugee camps were built and starving pandas were brought in. Grasses, meat, yams, and other foods were set out in panda territory. In addition, villagers were offered rewards for leading rescue teams to starving pandas.

News of the giant panda crisis reached the rest of the world. Newspapers and magazines ran articles about giant pandas

Researchers catch giant pandas with log traps. When the panda pulls on the meat bait, the door falls, trapping the panda inside.

and their dying bamboo. Soon, money began to pour in. Individuals and organisations from China and the rest of the world donated money to the panda rescue effort. Artists donated the proceeds from their work. In Shanghai, schoolchildren held a Panda Donation Day, while in the United States, children donated their money to the Pennies For Pandas fund.

While efforts to save the giant pandas were under way, biologists went out to survey the affected areas. When they had finished conducting their research, they realised that the bamboo dieback was not as bad as they had feared. Only one species of bamboo had died. Most of the giant pandas were able to simply switch their diet to a different kind of bamboo.

The 1983 crisis turned out to be far less serious than the one in the mid-1970s. Only a very few giant pandas died of starvation. What this crisis did, however, was show how much the people of the world care about saving giant pandas.

Giant Panda Plan

When the results of the 1985–1988 survey were counted, experts agreed that giant pandas must be protected, but there were many different ideas about how best to do this. American journalist Nancy Nash, known in China as "Miss Panda", brought the Chinese government and World Wildlife Fund together to form a plan to save the giant panda. In 1989 the Chinese Ministry of Forestry and World Wildlife Fund came up with a conservation plan for giant pandas. Both groups are now working hard to implement the plan. The plan's objectives are:

1) To maintain a **viable** population of wild giant pandas in their natural habitat.
2) To restore essential areas of giant panda habitat that have been damaged or destroyed by human activity. These areas include migration routes that allow the giant pandas to migrate during times of bamboo dieback, and to join other panda populations for mating.
3) To reduce logging and other forestry activities outside of the reserves in areas where giant pandas live.
4) To breed pandas in captivity so that wild pandas are not needed for breeding programmes and zoos.
5) To study giant pandas in more detail so that we can understand them better.

Conservation Symbol

Giant pandas have become a worldwide symbol for the need to preserve the variety of life on Earth. The panda's role as symbol has become known worldwide through the work of the international conservation organisation, WWF – World Wide Fund For Nature.

WWF was formed in 1961, when a group of scientists and media experts gathered to form an organisation that would raise money for nature conservation. The group based its work in Switzerland, near the scientific research-based conservation organisation known as IUCN – The World Conservation Union. Both groups agreed upon a common mission. They would "harness public opinion and educate the world about the necessity for conservation."

Meanwhile, a giant panda named Chi-Chi had arrived at London Zoo. Record numbers of people visited the zoo to see the furry black-and-white animal. Knowing they needed a recognisable symbol that would be popular around the world, WWF founders agreed that the giant panda would be an excellent choice. As WWF adopted the panda as its trademark, the animal began its career as a worldwide conservation symbol.

WWF was officially formed on September 11, 1961. Today, the initials WWF stand for World Wide Fund For Nature, except in North America, where the organisation is still called World Wildlife Fund.

The giant panda's furry body and seemingly huge black eyes give it an appeal that crosses language and cultural barriers.

Many Questions Remain...

The giant panda's fate is still uncertain. There are very few pandas left, and there are many questions about how to save them, or even if we should save them. What do you think about some of the questions being asked?

Should giant pandas be taken from the wild to stock captive breeding facilities?

Giant pandas in the wild are sometimes captured and placed in breeding facilities. Captive breeding helps preserve genetic diversity so that future panda populations will be viable. However, giant pandas breed much better in the wild than they do in captivity. In fact, a giant panda that is taken from the wild may never breed in captivity. Should potential giant panda parents ever be removed from the wild? If not, how can breeding programmes be maintained?

Should giant pandas be bred in captivity?

One goal of breeding pandas in captivity is to create a healthy population of animals that can eventually be released into the wild. However, wild giant pandas are losing so much of their natural habitat that soon there may not be enough suitable areas into which captive-bred animals can be released. If there is nowhere to release them, should facilities breed animals that may have to spend their entire lives in zoos?

There are about 15 giant pandas in zoos outside of China. Chinese zoos display another 90 captive animals.

Should people try to save the giant panda?

Some scientists believe the giant panda is a **remnant species**. This means the giant panda is probably becoming extinct naturally, not just because of human activity. Other scientists think the giant panda's problems are directly caused by humans. They believe that if the panda's declining status is the result of human activity, then people should do everything possible to save them. If the giant panda is a remnant species that is meant to become extinct, should people even try to save the species?

What You Can Do

We still do not know enough about giant pandas. By learning more, we can make better decisions about how to help them. Several conservation groups train biologists and develop plans and projects to study giant pandas. Write to them to find out how you can help.

Conservation Groups

GREAT BRITAIN

WWF – World Wide Fund for Nature
Panda House, Weyside Park
Godalming, Surrey
GU7 1XR
Phone: 01483 426444
www.wwf-uk.org

Environmental Investigation Agency (eia)
69-85 Old Street
London EC1V 9HX
Phone: 020 7490 7040
E-mail: eiauk@gn.apc.org
www.eia-international.org

*The **eia** conducts in-depth research and daring undercover investigations into illegal trade in endangered species.*

Pandas on the Internet

One of the places you can find out more about giant pandas is on the Internet. Visit the following sites, or try searching under the words "giant panda":

WWF
www.wwf.org

WWF Global Network
www.panda.org

National Geographic
www.nationalgeographic.com

The Bear Den
www.nature-net.com/bears

Planet Panda
planetpets.simplenet.com/plntpnda.htm

Twenty Fascinating Facts

1 Under its fur, the skin of a giant panda is black where its fur is black, and pink where its fur is white.

2 Giant pandas have a very good sense of smell. Even at night, they can find the best bamboo stalks by scent.

3 A giant panda's teeth are about seven times larger than human teeth.

4 Thick, waterproof fur allows giant pandas to sleep comfortably, even in the damp forest.

5 Giant pandas have evolved a special "thumb," which they use to hold bamboo stalks. This thumb is actually a wristbone.

6 Dens must be large enough for the mother giant panda to sit upright with her new cub.

7 Giant pandas have such powerful jaws that they can easily bite through a thick bamboo stalk. Humans would have trouble cutting the same stalk with an axe.

11 Gestation times for giant pandas vary due to a process called delayed implantation. This means that if a pregnant panda is not getting enough to eat, her cub will not start to grow.

12 The eyespots of a giant panda cub start out as circles. As the cub grows, the eyespots become shaped like a teardrop.

13 Giant pandas are solitary. The only time that they live with another panda is when a cub is raised by its mother, and when a male and female get together for a brief time during the mating season.

8 It can be very hard to see a giant panda in the wild because they are very shy, and their forested habitat is very thick. One biologist, who was looking for pandas on a daily basis, saw a panda only about once a month, even though 18 giant pandas lived in the area.

9 In the wild, giant pandas have been observed rolling on the ground and rubbing against rocks. Some pandas even pick up dirt and rub it over their bodies. Scientists do not know why giant pandas do this.

10 Giant panda mothers are 900 times larger than their newborn cubs.

14 Giant pandas use their tails as a kind of paintbrush to leave scent marks on trees or stumps.

15 Giant panda cubs are completely dependent on their mothers. They do not even open their eyes until they are about one month old.

16 The digestive system of a giant panda is not very efficient at using the bamboo the panda eats. Pandas cannot go for more than 5 or 6 hours without eating.

17 Giant pandas usually sit or lie down to eat. This means that all their paws are free for grasping bamboo stalks.

18 Although they are not good hunters, giant pandas will eat meat whenever they get the chance. Usually, pandas will eat dead animals that have been killed by another animal.

19 Each species of bamboo follows a cycle of growth, flowering, and dieback. During bamboo dieback, giant pandas must migrate to find another kind of bamboo to eat. This is a very difficult time for the pandas, and many of them die of starvation.

20 With just over 1,000 left in the world, giant pandas are on the verge of extinction. The most serious threats to giant panda populations come from poaching and habitat loss.

Glossary

camouflage: When an animal's appearance blends in with its environment so that it is very difficult to see.

carnivore: An animal that eats mainly the flesh and body parts of other animals.

carrion: The flesh of a dead animal.

delayed implantation: A process by which an unborn animal does not begin to grow in its mother's womb until some time after fertilisation.

dieback: When an entire species of bamboo reaches its flowering cycle and dies.

genes: The building blocks for making a living thing.

genetic testing: Tests that examine genes to discover the origin or development of a species.

gestation period: The length of time the female is pregnant with young.

hibernation: A period of time during the winter when certain animals' body temperature and heart rate drop dramatically in order to conserve energy.

home range: The entire area in which a giant panda lives.

migrate: To move from one area to another. A migration usually involves a large portion of a population.

opposable: A finger or thumb that can be placed against one or more of the other fingers on the same hand.

poach: To kill an animal illegally.

radio tracking: A method of study whereby biologists attach a special collar to an animal's neck. The collar sends out radio signals that the biologists use to keep track of the animal's movements.

remnant species: A species that is becoming extinct through natural processes.

scent marking: When a panda rubs itself on a stump or log to leave an odour that will tell other pandas it is in the area.

solitary: The state of living or being alone.

tranquilliser: A drug used to calm animals.

viable: Capable of living, growing, and reproducing. A viable population has enough animals to prevent each member from mating with closely related animals.

Suggested Reading

Angel, Heather. *Pandas*. Scotland: Colin Baxter Photography, 1998.

Bright, M. *Nature Watch: Bears and Pandas*. London: Lorenz Books, 2000.

De Beauregard, D. C. *Wildlife Alert*. London: Moonlight, 1989.

Fowler, Allan. *Giant Pandas*. Chicago: Children's Press, 1995.

Jin, Xugi. *Giant Panda*. London: Dent, 1986.

Kim, Melissa. *The Giant Panda*. London: Hutchinson, 1995.

Laidler, Keith and Liz. *Pandas*. London: BBC Books, 1992.

McClung, Robert. *Lili, A Giant Panda of Sichuan*. New York: Morrow Junior Books, 1988.

Rogers, Barbara Radcliffe. *Giant Pandas*. London: Headline, 1990.

Roots, Clive. *The Bamboo Bears*. London: Hale, 1991.

Schaller, George. *The Giant Pandas of Wolong*. Chicago: University of Chicago Press, 1985.
The Last Panda. Chicago: University of Chicago Press, 1993.

Schlein, M. *Animal World: Pandas*. London: Collins, 1990.

Taylor, David. *The Giant Panda*. London: Boxtree, 1990.

Ward, P. and Kynaston, S. *Bears of the World*. London: Blandford, 1995.

Willis, Terri. *Sichuan Panda Forests*. Texas: Raintree Steck-Vaughn, 1995.

Wonders of the World: *Sichuan Panda Forests*. Cherrytree Books, 1998.

Index